Make a New Friend in Jesus

PassAlong Arch® Books help you share Jesus with friends close to you and with children all around the world!

When you've enjoyed this story, pass it along to a friend. When your friend is finished, mail this book to the address below. Concordia Gospel Outreach promises to deliver your book to a boy or girl somewhere in the world to help him or her learn about Jesus.

Myself

My name _____

My address _____

_____

My PassAlong Friend

My name _____

My address _____

_____

When you're ready to give your PassAlong Arch® Book to a new friend who doesn't know about Jesus, mail it to

Concordia Gospel Outreach
3547 Indiana Avenue
St. Louis, MO 63118

PassAlong Series

God's Good Creation
Noah's Floating Zoo
Baby Moses' River Ride
Jonah's Fishy Adventure
Baby Jesus, Prince of Peace
Jesus Stills the Storm
Jesus' Big Picnic
God's Easter Plan

Jonah's Fishy Adventure

Jonah for Children

Carol Greene
Illustrated by Michelle Dorenkamp

CPH™
SAINT LOUIS

here was a town called Nineveh,
A large and wicked place.
And God said all that wickedness
Was staring in His face.

God chose a man called Jonah and
God said, "I want you to
Go tell those folks in Nineveh
I hate the things they do."

"Sounds like Nineveh's in big trouble!"

Jonah, go to Nineveh.
You know what you must say.
Jonah, go to Nineveh.
Set out this very day.

"Come on,
Jonah.
Move!"

But Jonah didn't want to go,
Although God's wish was plain.
"I'll run away from God," he thought.
"I'll take a boat to Spain."

To Joppa by the sea he dashed.
A ship was waiting there,
A ship for Tarshish. (That's in Spain.)
So Jonah paid his fare.

"What are you *doing*, Jonah?"

Jonah, what is wrong with you?
Your whole idea is odd.
Jonah, what is wrong with you?
You can't escape from God.

Then the ship sailed out to sea
And Jonah went below
To take a little nap. That's when
The wind began to blow.

That mighty wind came straight from God
And with it came a storm.
But Jonah didn't hear a thing.
He slumbered snug and warm.

"Trying to run away from God must be exhausting."

Wake up, Jonah! Don't you know?
Oh, don't you have a clue?
Wake up, Jonah! Don't you know
God's doing this for you?

"He's snoring!"

ZZZZ

Up above, the storm grew worse.
The crew began to shake.
"Our poor old ship can't take the strain
And soon she's going to break."

Quick they prayed to all their gods.
Their gods had ears of clay.
So the captain went below.
"Wake up there, Jonah. Pray!"

Jonah, aren't you sorry now?
  You've made those brave men cry.
  Jonah, aren't you sorry now?
  They think they're going to die.

"Shame on you, Jonah."

Then the men cast lots to learn
Whose fault the storm might be.
You can guess how that turned out.
"It's me," said Jonah. "Me.

"I was trying to run from God.
That wasn't very bright.
Toss me overboard, my friends,
And then you'll be all right."

"Way to go, Jonah!"

Jonah, what a price to pay.
You'll end up soaking wet.
Jonah, what a price to pay.
But God's not finished yet.

Splash, into the brine he went
And then he heard a *swish*.
"What was thaaa—" he cried as he
Was gulped down by a fish.

It was very dark and wet
And smelly there inside.
"Save me, God, and I'll obey,"
Poor soggy Jonah cried.

"He's in there.
I can hear him!"

Jonah, Jonah, say your prayers.
It's all that you can do.
Jonah, Jonah, say your prayers
And God will answer you.

"Listen to that Jonah pray!"

Three days later, up he came,
  Kerplop, upon the shore.
  "Go to Nineveh," said God.
  He had to say no more.

Jonah went to Nineveh.
  He preached. The people heard.
  "We will change our ways," they said.
  "We'll listen to God's Word."

"Yippee!"

Jonah, are you grumpy now
Because God let them live?
Jonah, are you grumpy now?
But God *wants* to forgive.

"Hey, Jonah.
Be happy!"

Anyplace is Nineveh
When folks have wicked ways.
But God's way still is to forgive.
It is! So give Him praise.

"That's very good news."